Bible
Puzzletime

SCRIPTURE UNION
130 City Road, London EC1V 2NJ

The puzzles in this book are based on the
Good News Bible
Many of them first appeared in the
Scripture Union publications
Quest and *Adventurers*

© Scripture Union 1987

First published 1987
Reprinted 1987, 1988
ISBN 0 86201 432 8

Printed by Spottiswoode Ballantyne, Printers Ltd

Meet Jesus

Use this code to find some people
who met Jesus.

a	b	c
d	e	f
g	h	i

j.	k.	.L
m.	.n.	.o
p.	q.	.r

v⧖t / ⧗u (s top, t right, v left, u bottom)

z⧗x / y (w top, x right, z left, y bottom)

┘ ⊐⌐⊐ ∨∏⊏
A MAN WHO
LE∧⌐⊐˙ ∏⊐⌐F
COULDN'T HEAR

∨E⊐⊐ ⊐⊐E⊐L⊐ ∨∏⊏
SOME PEOPLE WHO
∨⊐F⊐ ∏∧⊐⊐F∧
WERE HUNGRY

∨E⊐⊐ L∏⌐⌐F⊐⊐
SOME CHILDREN

┘ ⊐⌐⊐ ∨∏⊏
A MAN WHO
∨J∨ ∪L⌐⊐J
WAS BLIND

3

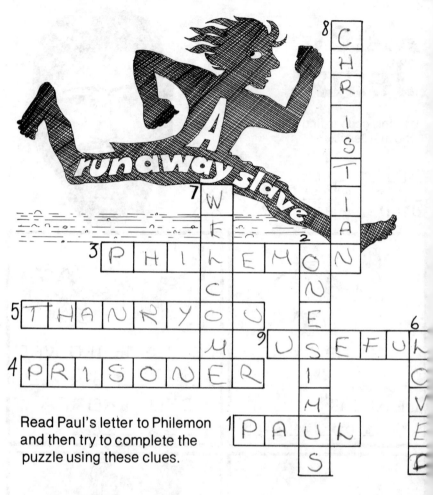

Read Paul's letter to Philemon and then try to complete the puzzle using these clues.

1 He wrote the letter.

2 The slave.

3 The slave's master.

4 Paul was a _____.

5 Paul always said — — to God for Philemon.

6 Paul had heard that Philemon — God's people.

7 Paul wanted Philemon to —' Onesimus.

8 Onesimus had become a —!

9 Onesimus means —.

IT'S A MIRACLE

Read the story in Mark 7:31–37, then decide what could go in the speech bubbles.

Colour in the shapes with dots to find a message that is amazing but true.

5

Missing!

What is missing in each of these pictures?

1. *Pedels*

2. *wire*

3. *words*

4.  *tail*

5. 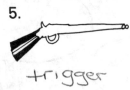 *trigger*

6.  *fillament*

Without Jesus, life is just as incomplete as one of these pictures.
Find out what he said by solving the puzzle. For example, B3 is
'that', found by following B across and 3 down.

	1	2	3	4
A	have	its	might	come
B	you	all	that	I
C	order	life	fullness	in

B4   A1   A4   C4   C1

I have come in order

B3   B1   A3   A1   C2

that you ~~order~~ might have life ;

C2   C4   B2   A2   C3

life in all its fullness

John 10:10

6

the missing sheep

Help the shepherd find his way through the maze to the lost sheep.

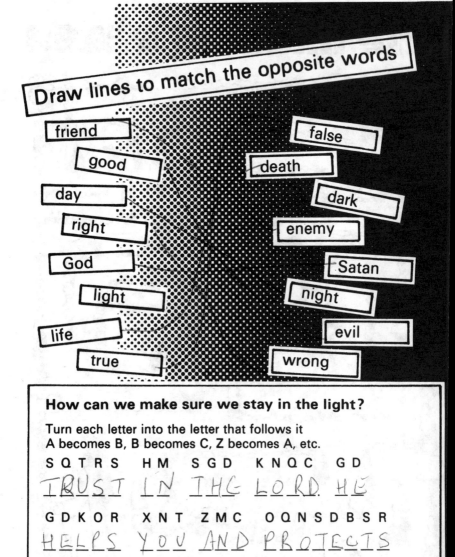

Draw lines to match the opposite words

friend

good

day

right

God

light

life

true

false

death

dark

enemy

Satan

night

evil

wrong

How can we make sure we stay in the light?

Turn each letter into the letter that follows it
A becomes B, B becomes C, Z becomes A, etc.

S Q T R S   H M   S G D   K N Q C   G D

TRUST IN THC LORD. HE

G D K O R   X N T   Z M C   O Q N S D B S R

HELPS YOU AND PROTECTS

X N T

YOU

Psalm 115:11

Jesus by the lakeside

Can you spot the eight differences between the two pictures?

The crossword grid shows:
E L I J A H
with crossing words including CHARIOT (2 across), JORDAN (down), STRUCK (3 down), CLOAK/TOWER, WHIR (6)

1. Which river dried up to let
   Elijah cross? (7)
2. What came between Elijah
   and Elisha? (11)
3. Elijah did this to the water (8).
4. This was Elijah's, until Elisha
   put it on (13).
5. Elisha received the _____ that God
   had given to Elijah (15).
6. Elijah was taken away by this (11).
7. This was making people ill until Elisha's miracle (19)
8. When Elijah went, Elisha did this (12)
9. Elisha waited here (18).
10. Elijah went here (11).
11. Elisha _____ saw Elijah again (12).
12. Fifty of these searched unsuccessfully for Elijah (15).
13. The poisonous water became _____ (22).

The numbers in brackets show you
which verse in 2 Kings 2 to look at.

Chariot of Fire

Mountain Cave

Take Elijah up the right path to reach
the cave at the top of Mount Sinai.

God's day... and God's house

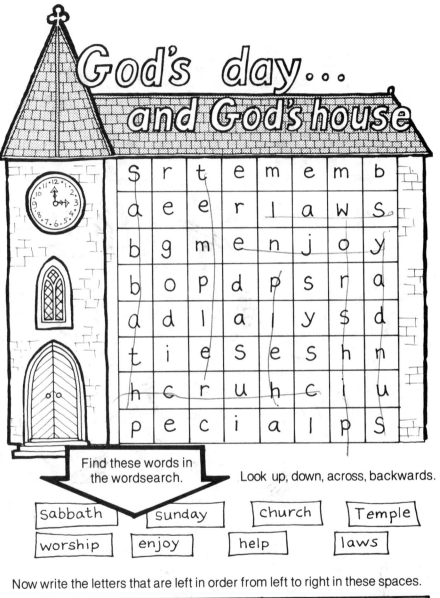

S	r	t	e	m	e	m	b
a	e	e	r	l	a	w	s
b	g	m	e	n	j	o	y
b	o	p	d	p	s	r	a
a	d	l	a	i	y	s	d
t	i	e	S	e	S	h	n
h	c	r	u	h	c	i	u
p	e	c	i	a	l	p	S

Find these words in the wordsearch.

Look up, down, across, backwards.

Sabbath   Sunday   church   Temple

worship   enjoy   help   laws

Now write the letters that are left in order from left to right in these spaces.

| R | E | M | E | M | B | E | R | | G | O | D | 'S |

| D | A | Y | | I | S | | B | E | C | I | A | L |

13

Find the other half of each cracker, and draw a line to join them together.

14

Goliath Identikit

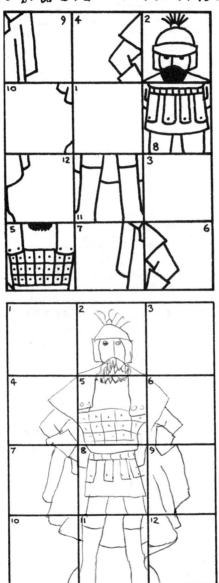

Draw the lines in the right squares and a giant will appear.

God saves Noah

Tick the right answer

Noah was saved because:

he was a good builder   a ☐

he trusted God   b ☑

he had read the Bible   c ☐
(Genesis 7:1)

Who went into the boat with Noah?

his family   d ☑

his friends   e ☐

his neighbours   f ☐
(Genesis 7:7)

How long did it rain?

4 days   g ☐

14 days   h ☐

40 days   i ☑
(Genesis 7:17)

God promised Noah:

that it would never rain again   j ☐

that he would never again destroy
all living beings by a flood.   k ☑

that there would be a drought   l ☐
(Genesis 8:15)

The sign of God's promise is:

a dove ☐ m   a raven ☐ n   a rainbow ☑ o

(Genesis 8:14, 15)

Easter Message

Sometimes it is hard to understand things.

What did Jesus tell his disciples? Work out the code, then check with Mark 9:30-32.

a	c	e	i	l	o	u
b	d	f	k	m	t	w

a = b, b = a etc.

k ukmm af ikmmfc
I WILL be KILLed
awo k ukmm dt lf
but I will come
abdi ot mkef.
back to life.

The disciples didn't understand what Jesus was saying and they were too frightened to ask.

We know that Jesus was talking about dying on the cross and rising to life again. When do we particularly remember this?

Working for Jesus

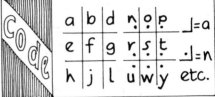

Code

a	b	d	n	o	p	⌐=a
e	f	g	r	s	t	⌐·=n
h	j	l	u	w	y	etc.

If we are working for Jesus we should:

⌐⌐⌐⌐· ⌐⌐⌐·⌐⌐⌐⌐·⌐·⌐⌐⌐·⌐⌐
HELP OTHER PEOPLE

□⌐⌐⌐⌐·⌐ ⌐⌐□·⌐□
FOLLOW JESUS.

⌐⌐⌐□⌐⌐·⌐⌐□·⌐□
TRUST JESUS.

⌐⌐⌐⌐·⌐⌐⌐⌐⌐□
TELL OTHERS

⌐⌐⌐·⌐⌐·⌐⌐□·⌐□
ABOUT JESUS.

⌐⌐⌐⌐·⌐ ⌐⌐⌐
OBEY GOD.

17

The Easter Story Luke 22 — 24

Answer these questions. Correct answers
lead to the next question.
Draw in your route to the star.

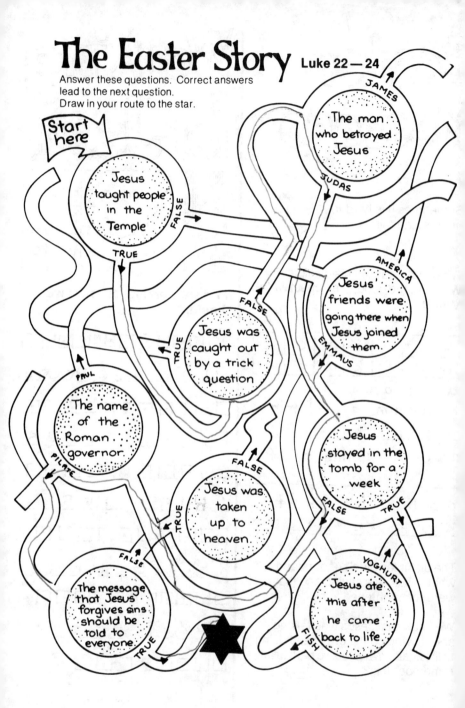

Start here

Jesus taught people in the Temple

The man who betrayed Jesus

JAMES

JUDAS

FALSE

TRUE

Jesus was caught out by a trick question

Jesus' friends were going there when Jesus joined them.

AMERICA

EMMAUS

FALSE

TRUE

The name of the Roman governor.

PAUL

PILATE

Jesus was taken up to heaven.

FALSE

TRUE

Jesus stayed in the tomb for a week

FALSE

TRUE

The message that Jesus forgives sins should to be told to everyone.

FALSE

TRUE

Jesus ate this after he came back to life.

YOGHURT

FISH

18

Th Good Sam ritan

Put these pictures in the right order to tell the story in Luke 9:25-37
For example, D = 1.

Sing to God

My first is in poem,

But never in song.

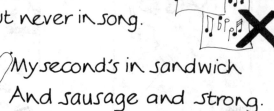

My second's in sandwich

And sausage and strong.

My third is the first
In the whole alphabet

My fourth is in lion and lemon
and let.

My fifth is the start of
two months' names

My sixth is in Quest
and also in same.

Put all six together and if you're not wrong
You've the name of a book full of poems and songs.

P	S	A	L	M	S
1	2	3	4	5	6

God's plan works out

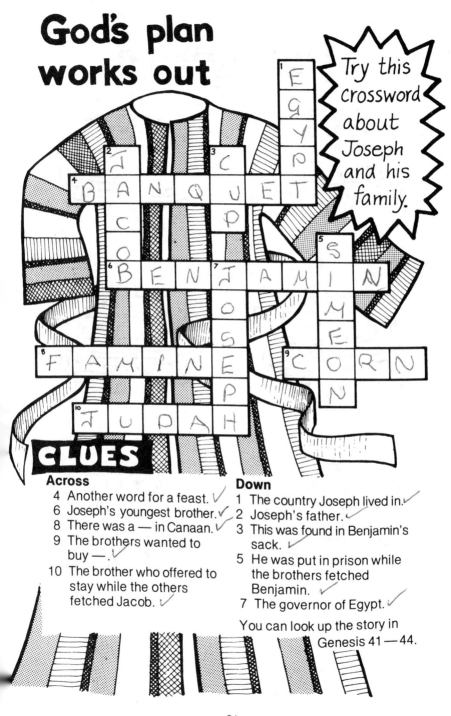

Try this crossword about Joseph and his family.

The crossword grid (about Joseph):

- 1 (Down): EGYPT
- 2 (Down): JACOB
- 3 (Down): CUP
- 4 (Across): BANQUET
- 5 (Down): SIMEON
- 6 (Across): BENJAMIN
- 7 (Down): JOSEPH
- 8 (Across): FAMINE
- 9 (Across): CORN
- 10 (Across): JUDAH

CLUES

Across
4 Another word for a feast.
6 Joseph's youngest brother.
8 There was a — in Canaan.
9 The brothers wanted to buy — .
10 The brother who offered to stay while the others fetched Jacob.

Down
1 The country Joseph lived in.
2 Joseph's father.
3 This was found in Benjamin's sack.
5 He was put in prison while the brothers fetched Benjamin.
7 The governor of Egypt.

You can look up the story in Genesis 41 — 44.

Two by Two

a.

b.

c.

d.

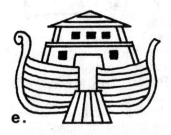

e.

f.

Which two pictures are identical?

B + E

Happy birthday Jesus!

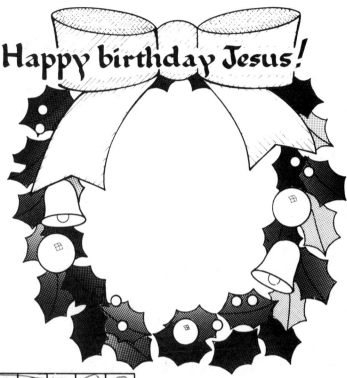

h	t	p	y	g	e	e	m
a	p	r	s	p	y	l	a
b	i	e	l	r	t	b	n
j	o	s	e	p	h	a	g
e	h	e	g	m	d	t	e
s	a	n	n	y	a	s	r
u	s	t	a	r	t	r	o
s	j	s	e	s	u	s	y

Can you find these words in this Christmas wordsearch?
Look up, down, forwards, backwards and diagonally.

~~Mary, Joseph, Jesus, angels, stable, manger, presents, star, Egypt.~~

Now write down the left over letters in order.

hAPPY
BIRTHDAY
to
Iesus!

Jesus

Finish decoding these facts from the Jesus file

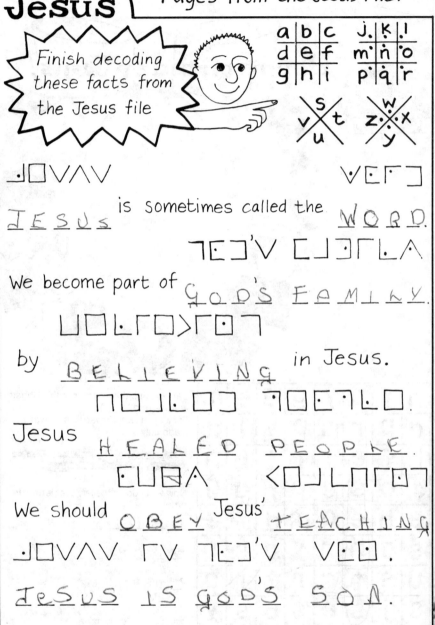

a	b	c		j.	k	l
d	e	f		m	n	o
g	h	i		p	q	r

s/v/u   t   w/z/x/y

JESUS is sometimes called the WORD.

We become part of GOD'S FAMILY.

by BELIEVING in Jesus.

Jesus HEALED PEOPLE.

We should OBEY Jesus' TEACHING

JESUS IS GOD'S SON.

Hard times for Joseph

Find six words connected with Joseph's story. Look across, down and diagonally.

1. robe
2. potiphar
3. Egypt
4. famine
5. dreams
6. Ring

p	a	d	b	c	d	e	f
o	g	h	r	i	j	k	l
t	m	n	o	e	p	f	a
i	k	i	n	g	a	a	v
p	r	s	t	y	u	m	w
h	x	y	z	p	a	i	s
a	b	c	d	t	e	n	f
r	o	b	e	g	h	e	i

Just for fun

You will need a calculator for this trick.

Type in the number of books in the Old Testament.
Multiply by the number of commandments God gave (Exodus 20).
Divide by the number of testaments that make up the Bible.
Subtract the number of gospels (look at the beginning of the New Testament).
Multiply by the number of men who visited Abraham (Genesis 18:2).
Multiply by the number of books in the Bible.
Press the equals key.
Turn the calculator upside-down.
What word have you made?

CODEBREAKER

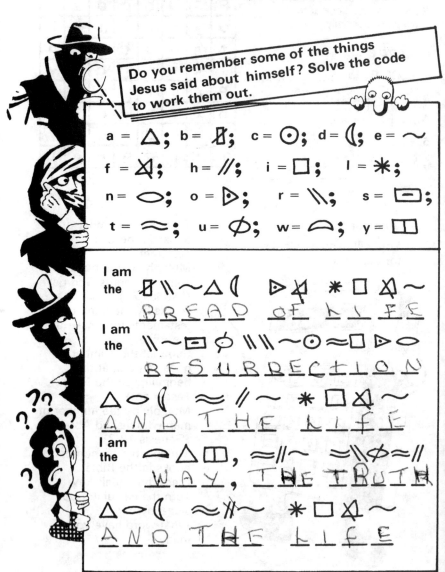

Do you remember some of the things Jesus said about himself? Solve the code to work them out.

a = △; b = ☒; c = ☉; d = (; e = ~

f = ☒; h = //; i = □; l = ✳;

n = ◠; o = ▷; r = \\; s = ▭;

t = ≈; u = ⊘; w = ◠; y = ▯

I am the BREAD OF LIFE

I am the RESURRECTION AND THE LIFE

I am the WAY, THE TRUTH AND THE LIFE

26

Here is Jesus in the Temple talking about why God sent him.

Can you find three squares that are exactly the same?

The great escape

Put a ✔ if the statement is right and a ✗ if it is wrong.

Baby Moses was hidden in some trees. Exodus 2:3 ✗	An Egyptian princess found Moses. Exodus 2:6 ✔	Moses had to run away from Egypt. Exodus 2:15 ✔
God spoke to Moses from a burning boat. Exodus 3:2 ✗	Aaron was Moses' brother. Exodus 4:14 ✔	The king of Egypt listened to God. Exodus 5:2 ✗
God punished the king of Egypt. Exodus 11:1 ✔	The Egyptians didn't try to cross the Red Sea. Exodus 14:23 ✗	God saved the Israelites. Exodus 14:30 ✔

MARCHING ROUND JERICHO

Can you spot seven differences between the two pictures?

A Special Promise

God made a special promise to Abram. Read
Genesis 17:1-8, then work out what it was.
(It tells you what the word 'ancestor' means.)

Write down the first letter of each word.

God promised that Abram

| W | O | U | L | D | | B | E | | T | H | E | | F | A | T | H | E | R |

| O | F | | M | A | N | Y | | N | A | T | I | O | N | S |

Abram had to

| O | B | E | Y | | G | O | D |

Let's learn from Jesus

Draw lines to join the first part of each sentence with the second.

thank you to God.

we should always say

to understand about God.

Jesus shows us

answers prayer.

God always

special to God.

The Holy Spirit helps us

God is like

God is always ready

My neighbour is

how to talk to God.

to forgive us when we say sorry.

love God.

a loving father.

We must

anyone who needs help.

We are all

Hard times, but The Jesus family grows

Can you fill in the missing words? The numbers give the chapters and verses in Acts.

Damascus

S _ _ _ _
preaches in
the synagogue
(9.20)

GALILEE

● **Caesarea**

Soul meets

J _ _ _ _ _
on his way to
Damascus
(9.1-8)

SAMARIA

Philip
P _ _ _ _ _ _ _
in every town
(8.40)

● **Ashdod**

S _ _ _ _ _ _ _ is stoned to
death and Christians have
to leave Jerusalem
(7.59-8.1)

● **Jerusalem**
The group of d _ _ _ _ _ _ _
grows bigger and bigger
as the apostles preach
(6.7)

The news
about
Jesus
spreads

JUDAEA

P _ _ _ _ _
meets a man
from
E _ _ _ _ _ _ _ _
● **Gaza** and tells him
about Jesus (8.27-35)
The
E _ _ _ _ _ _ _ _
man travels back
with the news

The church throughout J _ _ _ _ _,
G _ _ _ _ _ _ and S _ _ _ _ _ _ had a
time of peace. Through the help of

the H _ _ _ S _ _ _ _ _ it was
strengthened and grew in numbers,
as it lived in reverence for the

L _ _ _.
Acts 9, v.31 *Good News Bible*

Jacob and Esau

This crossword has the answers already filled in! Can you make up the clues? Genesis 28 will help.

```
7 R  a  c  H  e  L           2 J        1 I
      a                        a          s
3 E      4 R  e  b  e  c  c  a
  s         a                  o          a
5 L  a  b  a  n                b          c
  u
```

1 ....

2 ....

3 ....

4 ....

5 ....

6 ....

7 ....

The world God made

Use the code to find out some of the things in God's world.

⎅⌁⎅⎎⎎ WATER

⎎⎅⎅⎅ Food

⎎⎎⎅⎎⎎⎎ RIVERS

⎎⎅⎎⎎⎎⎎⎎ seasons

⎎⎎⎅⎎⎎⎎⎎ FLOWERS

⎎⎎⎎⎎⎎⎎⎎ animals

⎎⎎⎎⎎⎎⎎ birds

⎎⎎⎎ sun

⎎⎎⎎⎎⎎⎎⎎ People

Write down two ways you could help take care of God's world.

...... Don't drop litter ......

....

CITY SEARCH

Mary and Joseph have lost Jesus in Jerusalem. Help them to find their way through the streets to him.

God's Word

Join the right Bible reading to each verse that is written out.

1 Psalm 119 V.11

A
'God loved the world so much that he gave his only Son, so that everyone who believes in him may not die but have eternal life.'

2 Psalm 119 V.2

B
'Open my eyes so that I may see the wonderful truths in your law.'

3 Psalm 25 V.5

C
'Happy are those who follow his commands, who obey him with all their heart.'

D
'Your word is a lamp to guide me and a light for my path.'

4 Psalm 119 V.18

E
'I keep your law in my heart, so that I will not sin against you.'

F
'Teach me to live according to your truth, for you are my God who saves me. I always trust you.'

5 Psalm 119 V.105

6 John ch 3 V.16

THE HOLY SPIRIT

Galatians 5:22

The Holy Spirit wants to grow fruit in our lives. Can you find nine 'fruits' hidden in these letters? The first one is crossed off for you. Remember to look across and down.

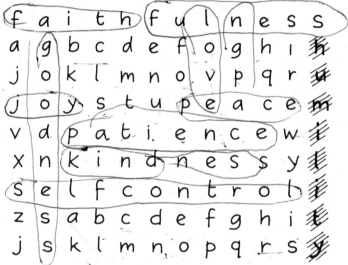

1
... used to be a magician and couldn't help making bad mistakes even after he became a Christian (*Acts 8:9*)

4 ... was an important leader of the Jews (*John 3:1*)

8
... was so poor that dogs licked him as he begged (*Luke 16:20*)*

5
... had once been a mad woman (*Luke 8:2*)

9
... was short and people hated him (*Luke 19:2–3*)

2
... was a hard-working woman (*Luke 10:40*)

6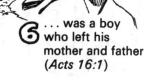
... was a boy who left his mother and father (*Acts 16:1*)

10 ... was a leader of the synagogue church (*Mark 5:22*)

3
... was a foreign woman who owned a materials shop (*Acts 16:14*)

7 ... was once blind and had to beg for money (*Mark 10:46*)

11
... was too scared to tell anyone he knew Jesus (*John 19:38*)

WHAT A MIXED BUNCH!

12 ... was a simple fisherman (*Mark 1:16*)

13 ... was a foreign army captain (*Acts 10:1*)

14 ... once hated Christians (*Acts 8:3*)

* in Jesus' parable

39

Animal Jungle

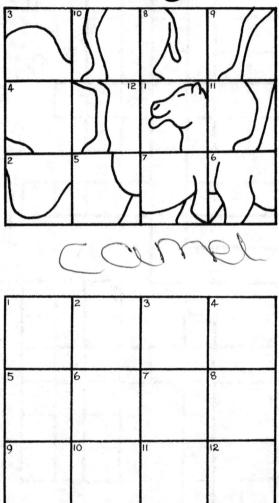

camel

Draw the lines in the right squares and an animal will appear.

Fame for a shepherd boy

Read 1 Samuel 16 and 17 for the story

1 The shepherd boy's name.
2 The king's name.
3 When the king felt ill, David played ___ for him.

4 David fought the giant ___.
5 The king offered to lend David his ___.
6 But David ___ God and didn't use it.

7 David wrote a song which says God is like a ___ who looks after us.

Now rearrange the shaded letters to spell the Bible book where we can find David's poems and songs.

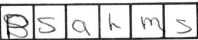

41

KING SOLOMON'S PRAYER

My first is in owl,
And also in wing

My second's in kindness
And also in king

My third is a letter that's
shaped like a snake.

My fourth is in David,
in duck and in drake

My fifth is a circle that goes
round and round

My sixth is a W that's
turned upside down.

Now write all six letters inside the six feet

The word you've
spelt out shows
the puzzle's
complete.
Solomon asked God for

W   I   S   D   O   M

RESCUE!

Read Exodus 14:19-22.

Ben, one of the Israelite boys, is being interviewed about what has happened. But he is so excited that he's got muddled up! Read Exodus 14:23-29 and correct the six mistakes in what he's said.

Fill in the missing letters

A str○ng w∩nd blΩw ∆ll n⊥ght. Th_e_ Isr_ _ _l_t_s w_r_ _bl_ t_ cr_ss th_ R_d S_ _ _ _n dry gr_ _nd w_th w_lls _f w_t_r _n b_th s_d_s.

We were crossing the Blue sea. I was very frightened when I saw the Persian soldiers coming after us. They had camels pulling their chariots. Suddenly the chariot wheels started sticking. Then Michael our leader, held out his foot. All the water started coming back. The sailors and their chariots were drowned. But we were safe!

God had rescued us.

Here is Jesus in his home. The pots on the shelves will tell you some things we know about young Jesus. Can you work out what they say?

A B D E G
I L N O P
R S T U W

44

45

The Lost Son

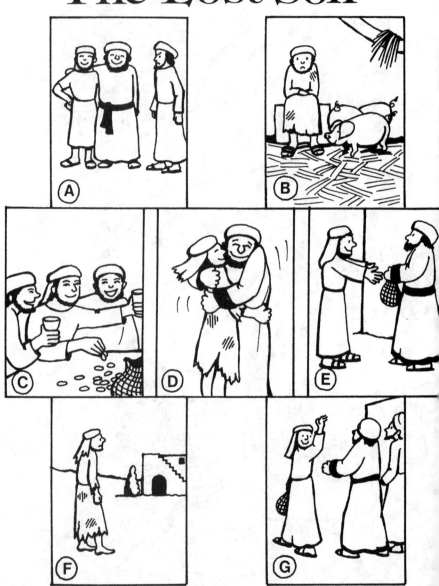

Put these pictures in the right order to tell the story in Luke 15:11-32.
To start you off, E = 1.

God's day

Write down the first letter of each object to find the missing words.

The **F O U R T H** commandment

Says we must keep one day special for God.

Jewish people call this day the  **S a b b a t h**

They worship God in a **S y n a g o g u e .**

The **S C R I P T U R E S**

are the Old Testament part of our Bible.

We keep **S u n d a y** as

a special day for God.

Some advice from Jesus straight to us

When you are giving a party . . .

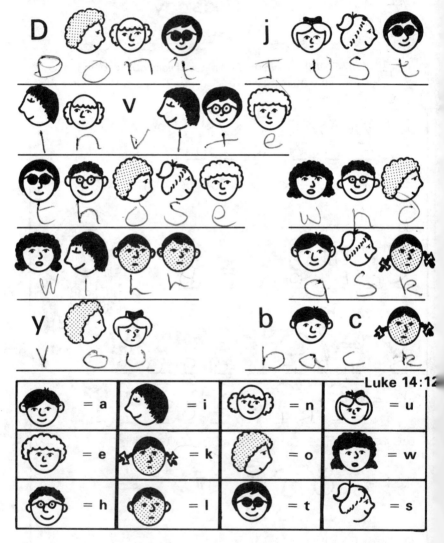

D o n ' t   j u s t

i n v i t e

t h o s e   w h o

w i t h   a s k

y o u   b a c k

Luke 14:12

= a		= i		= n		= u
= e		= k		= o		= w
= h		= l		= t		= s

SPOT THE DIFFERENCE

Jesus is asking his disciples to follow him for the first time. Judas must have seemed just like the other eleven. But there was a difference.

Can you find eight differences between the two pictures. Put a ring around each.

ELIJAH: the man who prayed.

All the answers to this crossword are names of people or places found in Elijah's story. Look at the Bible verses and write them in.

ACROSS

1 1 Kings 19:1
3 1 Kings 17:9
5 1 Kings 17:3
6 1 Kings 19:16
7 1 Kings 18:20
9 1 Kings 17:1
12 1 Kings 18:3
13 1 Kings 19:15

DOWN

1 1 Kings 19:3
2 1 Kings 19:3
5 1 Kings 18:19
8 1 Kings 18:1
9 1 Kings 19:17
10 1 Kings 19:16
11 1 Kings 19:8

Picturewords

Use the first letter of each picture to find a Bible message.

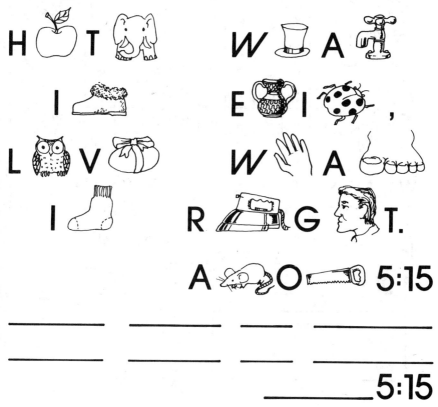

H🍎T🐘   W🎩A🚰

I👢   E🏺I🐞,

L🦉V🎀   W✋A🦶

I🧦   R📠G👤T.

A🐭O🪚 5:15

___ ___ ___

___ ___ ___

_____5:15

RUTH

Find seven names of people or places from the story of Ruth, hidden in the square.

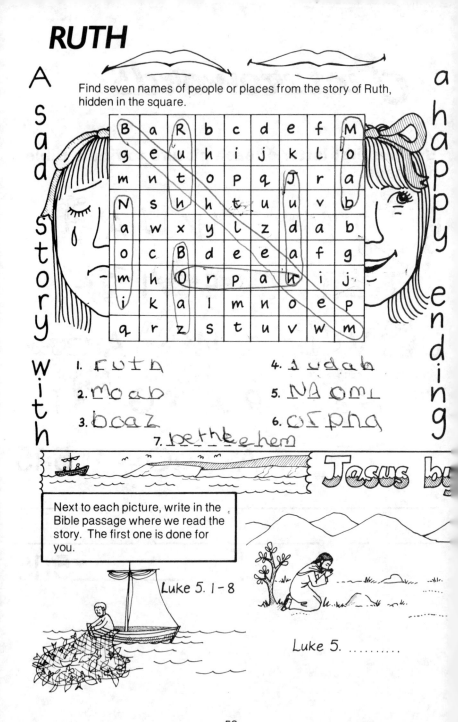

B	a	R	b	c	d	e	f	M
g	e	u	h	i	j	k	L	o
m	n	t	o	p	q	J	r	a
N	s	h	h	t	u	u	v	b
a	w	x	y	l	z	d	a	b
o	c	B	d	e	e	a	f	g
m	h	O	r	p	a	h	i	j
i	k	a	l	m	n	o	e	p
q	r	z	s	t	u	v	w	m

1. ruth
2. moab
3. boaz
4. judah
5. NAomi
6. orpha
7. bethlehem

Next to each picture, write in the Bible passage where we read the story. The first one is done for you.

Luke 5. 1-8

Luke 5. ....

52

People God helped

Unscramble the words to see who these people are and how God helped them.

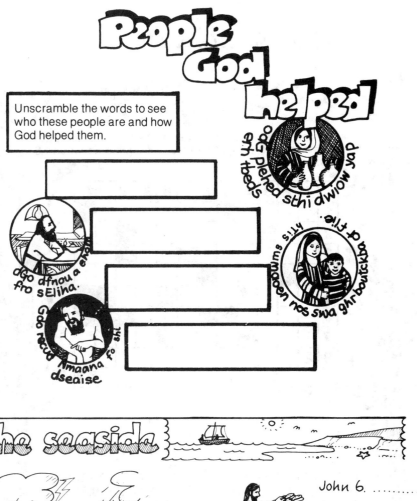

oGd pelhed sthi dwiow yap eht tbeds

dGo dfnou a erfoi fro sEliha.

Gdo recud nmaana fo shl dseaise

A ttris smuow woeen nos swa ghr bovtckba of ttie.

he seaside

John 6. . . . .

Luke 8. . . . .

A Verse to Learn

To find the memory verse put each letter in the right place on the grid. For instance, A is marked (1,6): that means 1 square down and 6 squares across, as shown.

	1	2	3	4	5	6	7	8	9	10	11	12
1						A						
2												
3												
4												;
5												
6												
7												
8	2											

5 : 17

A: (1,6) (4,1) (7,6) (8,10)
B: (4,7)
C: (3,1) (7,9) (8,2)
D: (2,9) (5,7)
E: (1,3) (1,11) (2,8) (3,9) (4,4) (4,8) (5,3) (6,4) (6,9) (7,2) (7,12)
G: (4,11) (6,1)
H: (1,2) (3,2) (3,8) (5,2) (6,8) (7,5) (8,8)
I: (2,1) (2,6) (3,4) (3,11) (4,9) (5,9) (8,5) (8,9)
J: (2,4)
L: (5,6)

M: (7,11)
N: (1,4) (1,7) (1,10) (2,7) (4,3) (4,10) (6,3) (7,1) (8,6) (8,11)
O: (1,9) (2,5) (2,12) (5,5) (6,2) (7,10) (8,3)
R: (3,3) (8,4)
S: (2,2) (3,5) (3,12) (5,10) (7,7) (8,12)
T: (2,11) (3,6) (5,1) (6,7) (8,7)
W: (1,1) (4,5) (7,3)
Y: (1,8)

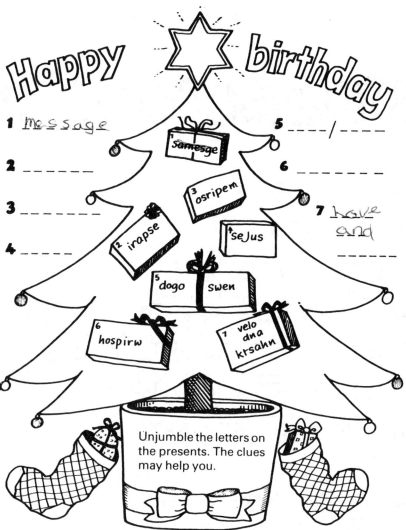

Happy ✦ birthday

1 message

2 _ _ _ _ _ _

3 _ _ _ _ _ _ _

4 _ _ _ _ _

5 _ _ _ _ / _ _ _ _

6 _ _ _ _ _ _ _

7 have and _ _ _ _ _ _

Presents on the tree:

1 Samesge

2 irapse

3 osripem

4 seJus

5 dogo swen

6 hospirw

7 velo dna ktrsahn

Unjumble the letters on the presents. The clues may help you.

1 The angel gave an important one to Mary.

2 Mary gave this to God.

3 God gave this to Abraham.

4 God's gift to us.

5 The angels gave this to the shepherds.

6 The wise men came to – Jesus.

7 What can we give to Jesus?

BRAINBUSTER?

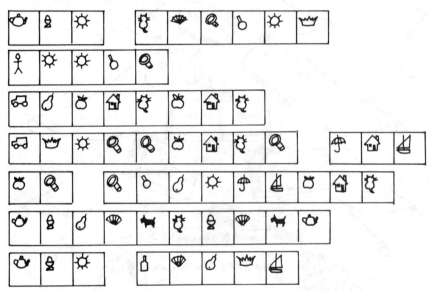

Colossians 1:6

Match the symbols to work out the code

Spot the Pots

Which two pictures are identical?

4

Jacob and Esau

Read the story in Genesis 27:1-29.

Use the picture clues to fill in the right names.

Isaac	Rebecca
Esau	Jacob

When Isaac grew old, he became blind. Isaac asked his elder son, Esau, to kill an animal and cook it for him. Isaac said he would give Esau his blessing. Rebecca was listening. She told her younger son Jacob to get two goats. Rebecca cooked them for Isaac. Jacob took the food to Isaac and pretended to be Esau. Isaac was tricked and gave Jacob his blessing instead of Esau.

Paul Puzzle

Solve the clues and read downwards to find Paul's
special responsibility.

1. A riot took place here (Acts 19:23)
2. Jesus wanted Paul to declare this (Acts 20:24)
3. They all did this when Paul left (Acts 20:37)
4. Who told Paul to go to Jerusalem? (Acts 20:22)
5. Who sent a message to Ephesus? (Acts 20:17)
6. What false goddess was the cause of the riot? (Acts 19:24)
7. Paul did this when they had finished (Acts 20:36)
8. What did Paul say to his friends? (Acts 20:1)
9. Where did Paul go to? (Acts 20:1)

Paul's job was to   the Christians.

Answers to Puzzles

page 3   A man who couldn't hear. Some people who were hungry. Some children. A man who was blind.

page 4   1 Paul. 2 Onesimus. 3 Philemon. 4 prisoner. 5 thank you. 6 loved. 7 welcome. 8 Christian. 9 useful.

page 5   Jesus heals.

page 6   1 pedals. 2 wire. 3 words. 4 tail. 5 trigger. 6 filament.
I have come in order that you might have life in all its fullness.

page 8   friend/enemy. good/evil. day/night. right/wrong. God/Satan. light/dark. life/death. true/false.
Trust in the Lord. He helps you and protects you.

page 9

pages 10/11   1 Jordan. 2 chariot. 3 struck. 4 cloak. 5 power. 6 whirlwind. 7 water. 8 cried. 9 Jericho. 10 heaven. 11 never. 12 prophets. 13 pure.

page 13

s	r	t	e	m	e	m	b
a	e	e	r	t	a	u	s
b	g	m	o	n	j	o	y
b	o	p	d	s	r	s	d
a	d	a	y	y	s	d	
l	i	e	s	e	s	h	
	g	r	u		g		u
p	e	c	i	a	l	p	s

Remember God's day is special.

page 14   Mary remembered everything the shepherds said. Herod had some unusual visitors. The shepherds hurried to Bethlehem. The visitors from the East brought unusual gifts. The angels sang praises to God. Joseph obeyed God's instructions. God sent his son to be our saviour.

page 16   b, d, i, k, o.

page 17   I will be killed but I will come back to life.
Help other people follow Jesus. Trust Jesus. Tell others about Jesus. Obey God.

page 18

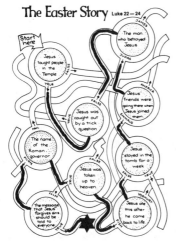

page 19   D = 1, A = 2, F = 3, B = 4, G = 5, E = 6, C = 7.

page 20   Psalms.

page 21   Across.   4 banquet.   6 Benjamin.   8 famine.   9 corn.
10 Judah.
Down.   1 Egypt.   2 Jacob.   3 cup.   5 Simeon.
7 Joseph.

page 22   b and e.

page 23

h	t	p	y	g	e	e	m
a	p	r	s	p	y		a
b	i	e		r	t	b	n
t	o	s	e	p	h	a	g
e	h	e	g	m	d	t	e
s	a	n	n	y	a	s	r
u	s	t	a	r	t	r	o
s	j	s	e	s	u	s	y

Happy birthday to Jesus!

page 24   Jesus is sometimes called the Word. We become part of God's family by believing in Jesus. Jesus healed people. We should obey Jesus' teaching. Jesus is God's son.

page 25   Robe, Potiphar, king, Egypt, dream, famine.
Bible.

page 26   I am the bread of life. I am the resurrection and the life.
I am the way, the truth and the life.

page 27   2F,   4A,   6F.

page 28   top row: X, ✓, ✓. middle row: X, ✓, X. bottom row: ✓, X, ✓.

page 29

page 30   God promised that Abram would be the father of many nations.
Abram had to obey God.

page 31   Jesus shows us how to talk to God. We should always say
thank you to God. God always answers prayer. The
Holy Spirit helps us to understand about God. God is always
ready to forgive us when we say sorry. My neighbour is
anyone who needs help. We must love God. We are all
special to God. God is like a loving father.

page 32   Saul preaches in the synagogue. Saul meets Jesus on his way
to Damascus. Philip preached in every town. Stephen is
stoned to death and Christians have to leave Jerusalem. The
group of disciples grows bigger and bigger. Philip meets a
man from Ethiopia and tells him about Jesus. The Ethiopian
man travels back with the news.
The church throughout Judaea, Galilee and Samaria had a
time of peace. Through the help of the Holy Spirit it was
strengthened and grew in numbers, as it lived in reverence for
the Lord.

page 33   1 Jacob and Esau's father.   2 He made bean soup.
3 He was a hunter.   4 Jacob and Esau's mother.
5 Jacob's uncle.   6 Where Jacob's uncle lived.   7 Jacob
married her.

page 34   water, flowers, animals, food, birds, rivers, sun, seasons,
people.

page 36   A = 6, B = 4, C = 2, D = 5, E = 1, F = 3.

page 37	humility, love, joy, peace, patience, kindness, goodness, faithfulness, self-control.
pages 38/39	1 Simon. 2 Martha. 3 Lydia. 4 Nicodemus. 5 Mary. 6 Timothy. 7 Bartimaeus. 8 Lazarus. 9 Zacchaeus. 10 Jairus. 11 Joseph. 12 Andrew. 13 Cornelius. 14 Saul.
page 41	1 David. 2 Saul. 3 music. 4 Goliath. 5 armour. 6 trusted. 7 shepherd. Psalms.
page 42	wisdom.
page 43	A strong wind blew all night. The Israelites were able to cross the Red Sea on dry ground with walls of water on both sides. (wrong word/right word) Blue/Red Sea. Persian/Egyptian soldiers. camels/horses. Michael/Moses. foot/hand. sailors/drivers.
pages 44/45	wise, obedient, growing strong, popular.
page 46	E = 1, G = 2, C = 3, B = 4, F = 5, D = 6, A = 7.
page 47	fourth, sabbath, synagogue, scriptures, Sunday.
page 48	Don't just invite those who will ask you back.
page 49	

page 50	Across. 1 Jezebel. 3 Sidon. 5 Cherith. 6 Nimshi. 7 Baal. 9 Elijah. 12 Obadiah. 13 Hazael. Down. 1 Judah. 2 Beersheba. 5 Carmel. 8 Ahab. 9 Elisha. 10 Jehu. 11 Sinai.
page 51	Hate what is evil, love what is right. Amos 5:15
page 52	1 Ruth. 2 Moab. 3 Boaz. 4 Naomi. 5 Judah. 6 Orpah. 7 Bethlehem. Luke 5:1-8, Luke 5:16, Luke 8:22-25, John 6;1-13.
page 53	God helped this widow pay her debts. God found a home for Elisha. This woman's son was brought back to life. God cured Naaman of his diseases.
page 54	When anyone is joined to Christ he is a new being: the old is gone, the new has come. 2 Corinthians 5:17.
page 55	1 message. 2 praise. 3 promise. 4 Jesus. 5 good news. 6 worship. 7 love and thanks.
page 56	The gospel keeps bringing blessings and is spreading throughout the world.
page 57	c and f.
page 58	Isaac, Isaac, Esau, Isaac, Esau, Rebecca, Jacob, Rebecca, Isaac, Jacob, Isaac, Esau, Isaac, Jacob, Esau.
page 59	1 Ephesus. 2 good news. 3 cried. 4 Holy Spirit. 5 Paul. 6 Artemis. 7 prayed. 8 goodbye. 9 Macedonia. Paul's job was to encourage the Christians.